FIGURES IN CHINA'S SPACE INDUSTRY

Who is Huang Weilu?

www.royalcollins.com

FIGURES IN CHINA'S SPACE INDUSTRY

Who is Huang Weilu?

By Ye Qiang and Dong Pingping

Books Beyond Boundaries

ROYAL COLLINS

Huang Weilu (December 18, 1916–November 23, 2011) was a famous rocket and missile scientist from Wuhu, a small city in China's Anhui Province. Huang's most important contribution was the invention of solid-propellant strategic missiles, and he made a major breakthrough in the techniques of underwater launches and solid-propellant engine building. That made him a leading character in launching solid-propellant rockets and missiles in China. These accomplishments titled Huang one of the founding fathers of China's space industry and won him the "Two Bombs, One Satellite" Medal of Merit.* But his work was also influential outside of China, as he was honored with fellowships both in the Chinese Academy of Science and the International Academy of Astronautics.

---

* The "Two Bombs, One Satellite" was a very important nuclear and space project of China. The "Two Bombs" are China's first nuclear bomb and the first group of missiles. The "One Satellite" is China's first artificial satellite and geostationary satellite. A group of outstanding scientists worked very hard for decades to make this happen, as you'll see in the story of Huang Weilu and others. And these scientists who have devoted their whole life to the nuclear and space industry of China were awarded the "Two Bombs, One Satellite" Meritorious Medals. An extremely high honor for themselves and for all Chinese people to remember their great work!

Huang grew up with three brothers and sisters, and so his parents were always kept busy and couldn't pay attention to him very often. Having plenty of time to be with himself, little Huang developed a strong character and a strong mind, as he loved spending this time thinking. His ideas were also quite unusual. For example, when he saw other children playing with bamboo dragonflies and competing against each other to see who made it to the highest and farthest, little Huang was thinking how he could make a flying bomb out of this common toy!

"If I could attach several bamboo dragonflies together and make them work together, add a rubber band to it so that I can shoot it off, put fireworks under it, use incense as a lead wire, calculate the time so that it can explode where I want it to...isn't it a flying bomb already?" It is not surprising that a boy like Huang, with such creativity in making bombs, would grow up to be an expert in building missiles, is it?

His love for thinking made him a clever and hardworking student in school. In Fall 1933, he got excellent grades in the admission tests and was accepted by the well-known Yangzhou High School, which he later said was a milestone in his life. When he graduated, however, he suddenly fell ill and lost his chance to apply for National Tsing Hua University (now called Tsinghua University). Fortunately, he soon recovered and was successfully accepted both by National Central University and National Chekiang University (now called Zhejiang University), thanks to the good education he received in high school.

Disaster fell upon the country on July 7, 1937. The world was astonished by the Japanese army's sudden military attack at the Marco Polo Bridge in China's Hebei Province. The Marco Polo Bridge Incident then led to the outbreak of the Second Sino-Japanese War. The National Central University, where Huang was then studying, was forced to move its campus and students to Chongqing in the southwest interior of China.

In the letters sent from home, his father told him, "Our country is now under attack, and that is because our country is weak. You, my boy, must study hard so that one day you could help to make it strong." Young Huang kept these words in his heart as they reminded him of his resolution to save his country.

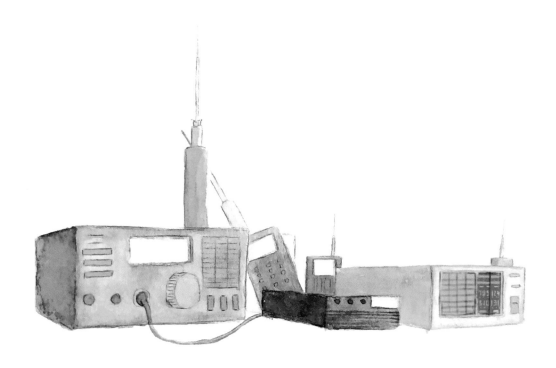

In August 1940, Huang finished his four-year study at the university as an outstanding graduate. He stayed in Chongqing and started working in the local Central Radio Appliance Factory under the National Resource Commission.

Huang worked in the factory for three years. The more he understood about his job, the more he realized how useless it was in saving China from her miserable state. "I must study more useful things in other countries," he thought to himself, "and then I can help my country with what I've learned." He started looking for all kinds of opportunities to go abroad, and luckily, he was able to go to the UK where he studied radio electronics at Imperial College London.

After completing his study in the UK in four years, Huang returned to his motherland only to find her still suffering from wars and poverty. Huang knew that time had come for him to make use of his knowledge and help his country. His eagerness to save China with science burned in him like fire.

13

Such eagerness and devotion to his home country were also passed on to his children. "Nothing is more important than your country," he told them. One night, Huang was working on an equation in his room. "Daddy!" his daughter called as she ran in. Huang quickly put the piece of paper with the equation written on it under some books.

"Yes, baby?" he asked, when he was sure his work wouldn't be messed up by the kid, who was also used to her father's action.

The little girl asked, "Daddy, what are we going to do if our country is at war?"

Huang looked at her and answered, "It won't happen. But remember, whatever happens, you should always think about your country, what is to be done with our country."

At that time, Huang was working on liquid-propellant missiles in the Fifth Academy of the Ministry of National Defense, but food was extremely sparse, and the family never had much to eat. Thin corn soup and old dry potatoes were on the table for every meal, every day. The dry potatoes had a foul smell and tasted like cement in the mouth. The children hated it and said they felt like eating limestones. When his children complained, Huang would finish his "limestones" first and then trade for theirs with his corn soup. His wife was very worried and told him he would get a stomachache eating too much of it, but he just laughed it off.

What his wife was worried about became real after all. Already under intense pressure working on the missile project day after night, his health became even worse, eating so many dry potatoes, which eventually gave him a bad stomach illness. In the daytime, he had to take pills to kill the pain. But at night, it was more difficult, and he was often kept awake by the terrible pain. He had to keep rubbing his stomach or keep pushing at it really hard to try to get over it. Sometime later, holes started to show up in his nightshirt where he used to rub and push.

19

Fortunately, his efforts all paid off and his pain was greatly relieved when the good news came on June 29, 1964, that the launching of Dongfeng II missile had succeeded! It was probably impossible for others to ever imagine how much hardship and suffering that the scientists in the Fifth Academy like Huang had gone through, having to build a whole new rocket from scratch and without any help from other countries.

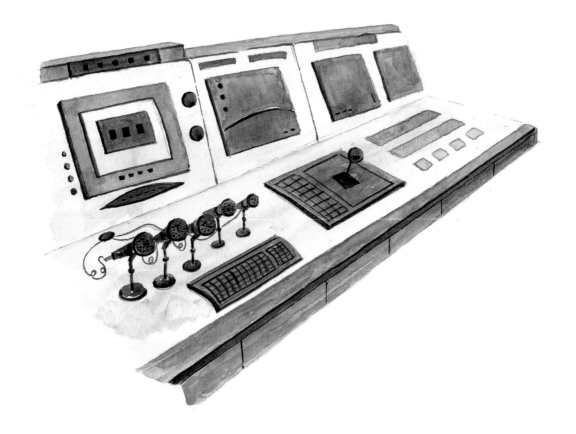

Of course, things didn't always go smoothly, and different kinds of unexpected incidents may happen at any time. For example, early on the morning of June 17, 1981, two minutes before the launch of China's solid-propellant submarine-to-ground missile, something about the missile suddenly appeared strange. Everyone was alarmed and didn't know what it meant. Huang quickly became calm and asked the scientists at the launch site about the conditions of the missile. Based on their answers, he understood that the problem was not serious and immediately gave the order to launch the missile. The ground shook as the missile soared into heaven. The launch was successful!

Four years later, with a deafening noise, another new missile designed by Huang—a ground-vehicle-based telemetry missile—succeeded in its test launch. The scientist has now carried out his resolution as a young man to make his country strong.

In his everyday work among his fellow scientists, Huang has always been a careful and reliable leader, and he could quickly detect the cause of a problem while others were still confused. Once, with a Dongfeng V missile, something would always go wrong during its first and second stage separation process. For days, the crew members wondered about the reason for this problem. Then Huang arrived. After examining the site carefully, he found out that it was not the problem with the missile itself; rather, it was because an operator had unplugged a switch by accident. He solved the problem right away!

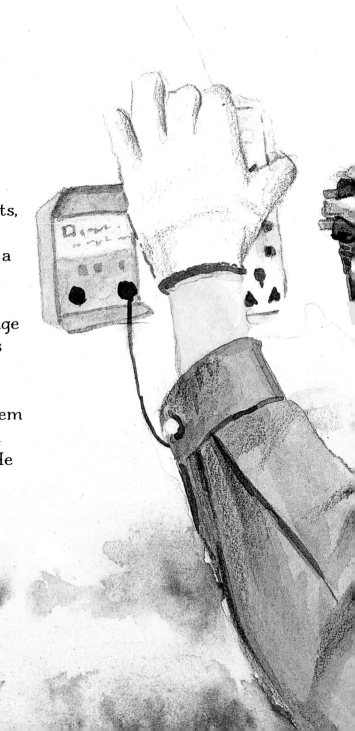

In July 2011, a summer camp about the "Two Bombs, One Satellite" took place at the University of South China, and the students craved the opportunity to talk to Huang, who was already an old man and suffering from severe illness. But when he heard the wish of the children, he happily went to the camp site and communicated with the students. In the end, with shaking hands, he wrote the words "Pass down the spirit of Two Bombs, One Satellite, take up the responsibility of making your country strong" for the students—the last brushwork he did in his life.

Four months later, on the night of November 23, 2011, the great scientist Huang Weilu passed away in Beijing at the age of 95.

27

About the Authors

YE QIANG studied oil painting at Sichuan Fine Arts Institute. After graduating in 2001, he continued to teach in the Institute until 2008. Since then, he's been teaching as an Associate Professor in the Department of New Media Art and Design at Beihang University (Beijing University of Aeronautics and Astronautics). Ye's paintings have been displayed in hundreds of national and international exhibitions, and he has held solo exhibitions in galleries, including the Shanghai Art Museum, six times. Ye's paintings and scholarship can be found in more than 20 academic journals and monographs, such as *Art Observation*, *Art China*, *History to Chinese Oil Painting*, and more. He has also published seven textbooks, including *Basic Techniques in Drawing*, *Basic Techniques in Coloring*, and *A Brief Introduction in Abstract Painting Languages*.

DONG PINGPING is Vice-Secretary of the Party Committee and a member of the Supervisory Commission of the Department of New Media Art and Design at Beihang University.

Figures in China's Space Industry:
Who is Huang Weilu?

Written by Ye Qiang and Dong Pingping

First published in 2022 by Royal Collins Publishing Group Inc.
Groupe Publication Royal Collins Inc.
BKM Royalcollins Publishers Private Limited

Headquarters: 550-555 boul. René-Lévesque O Montréal (Québec) H2Z1B1 Canada
India office: 805 Hemkunt House, 8th Floor, Rajendra Place, New Delhi 110 008

ISBN: 978-1-4878-0892-1

To find out more about our publications, please visit www.royalcollins.com.